INTÉRIEUR D'UN ÉDIFICE, À KABAH.
Yucatan
INTERIOR OF AN EDIFICE, AT KABAH.
Yucatan

The houses were well built, with balconied windows, and many had two stories.
The streets were clean, and many people in them well dressed, animated, and cheerful in
appearance; calèches fancifully painted and curtained, having ladies in
them handsomely dressed, without hats, and their hair ornamented with flowers, gave it an air
of gaiety and beauty that, after the somber towns through which we
had passed, was fascinating and almost poetic.
—Author and explorer John L. Stephens, upon entering Mérida around 1840,
from Incidents of Travel in Yucatán *(1843)*

CASA MEXICO

 At Home in Mérida and the Yucatán

ANNIE KELLY

PHOTOGRAPHY BY TIM STREET-PORTER

RIZZOLI
NEW YORK

New York · Paris · London · Milan

CONTENTS

INTRODUCTION

If you could travel in Mexico back in time five hundred years, the town of Mérida—then known by its Mayan name of T'ho—would already be stretched out on the low, flat Yucatán plain. Today, its busy streets look like a typical cheerful and colorful Mexican metropolis, but this small city—considered to be one of the oldest continually occupied settlements in the Americas—also has an otherworldly character, and, thanks to the Mayans, an even richer cultural heritage than most other towns dating from this period. Colonized over 470 years ago by the Spanish adventurer Francisco de Montejo, today Mérida has a historic center that is one of the largest in Mexico. To solidify Spanish control of the city, all the surrounding pyramids were torn down, and their huge stone blocks were used as the foundation for what is today the oldest cathedral on the North American continent—the Cathedral of San Ildefonso, which was finished in 1598. This somewhat weather-beaten and venerable edifice is found on the main plaza next to several other historic buildings, including the Casa de Montejo of 1549, the grand former home of de Montejo, who is also considered the conqueror of the entire Yucatán Peninsula. Many of Mérida's original arched town gates can be seen in the earliest parts of the city. Mérida is still the cultural and financial capital of the region, and for a brief period in the late nineteenth century, thanks to the production of sisal, it was one of the richest towns in Mexico. As a result, a treasure trove of large-scale houses remains, many with original architectural features dating from a hundred years ago or more.

Today, a new breed of Yucatecan is moving into many of the buildings, renovating and restoring them to create full-time or even second or third homes. Hailing from Mexico City, Europe, Los Angeles, and New York,

this rapidly growing community of artists, sculptors, designers, and architects is inspired by the skill and craftsmanship of the local Mayans as well as their desire to build a more adventurous and colorful life here on the Yucatán Peninsula.

A lively food culture has also recently sprung up in the region, and on Saturday mornings in Mérida, many cooking enthusiasts can be found at the local Slow Food market buying regional produce like quail eggs and homegrown honey, and even earthworm-filled compost. Inspired by local Yucatecan dishes, which are distinctly regional, restaurant-owner chefs visit from all over the United States and Mexico, among them cooks from Rosetta in Mexico City and Grace in Chicago. David Sterling, who moved from New York over thirteen years ago, wrote the comprehensive Yucatán cookbook *Yucatán: Recipes from a Culinary Expedition*, which won the James Beard Foundation Best Cookbook of the Year award in 2015. Food author and chef Jeremiah Tower came for a visit several years ago and stayed, mainly because he fell in love with the impressively wide variety of local Mayan street food, including delicious tortilla-based *panuchos*, *salbutes*, and *esquites*—cups of corn served with cream, chile powder, and lime juice.

Residential Mérida reveals itself slowly to the visitor once you penetrate its defenses. The town is full of surprises. Indoor proportions are often huge, with twenty-foot-high ceilings and doors that open to reveal enfilades of tiled room after room. Metal hooks are built into almost every wall, spaced perfectly for hanging hammocks; these make bedrooms very informal and are comfortable to sleep in during hot evenings.

Opposite, top: A detail of the ancient front door of the Cathedral of San Ildefonso, completed in 1598. Opposite, bottom: The main town square of Mérida. Above, top: A natural fiber work by local sculptor Marcela Díaz installed at the Fundación des Artistas in Mérida. Above, middle: A plate of panuchos, *a local dish that is a specialty of the Hacienda Petac. Above, bottom: The traditional bed of the Yucatán—a coiled hammock hanging from hooks in the wall.*

Above, top: Dancing the jarana *in Mérida. Above, middle: The pre-Columbian ruins of Edzna, a Mayan temple in Campeche. Above, bottom: The dramatic facade of Hacienda Petac.*

About a twenty-mile-drive inland from the sea, Mérida is relatively protected from the annual hurricanes that sweep through the Caribbean. As a precaution, its houses are mostly compact one-story buildings, with gardens defined and sheltered within inner high-walled private courtyards. Outdoor life is either lived inside these family compounds or more publicly in the numerous town squares. From the buzzing markets at Mercado Lucas de Gálvez and dancers performing the Yucatecan *jarana* in the Parque Santa Lucía to the *vaquería* performed by the Ballet Folklorico de Mérida in front of the Municipal Palace, Mérida is a town full of color and movement.

We fell in love with the Yucatán over twenty years ago when we toured the nearby iconic pre-Columbian pyramids Chichen Itza and Uxmal. Today, the whole region has grown into a fashionable and popular destination, constantly featured in a wide variety of travel and design articles in newspapers and magazines all over the world. We found it most expeditious to begin the photography for this book in Mérida, and then use the town as a base to travel around the rest of the Yucatán to explore the contemporary evolution of Mexican interior design and exterior decoration, which, thanks to skilled local craftsmen and artisans, are ever-changing, always joyful, and deeply inspirational.

We photographed two very different haciendas: the seventeenth-century Hacienda Petac, sensitively restored by Josefina Larraín Lagos and her partner, architect Salvador Reyes Ríos; and the brand new Plantel

Matilde, an adventurous modern hacienda by architect Arcadio Marín, built for his brother, the sculptor Javier Marín. Near the village of San Antonio Sac Chich, it opens up like a modern-day acropolis and takes its name from the field it is built on.

For some people, the small town of Valladolid, which is on the way to the beach resort of Tulum, is a peaceful alternative to the much larger city of Mérida. Here, Nicolas Malleville and Francesca Bonato originally just opened a small store and guest hotel, but they made their home there temporarily after a hurricane swept through their beachside property in Tulum. They loved Valladolid's quiet and colorful beauty, and decided to stay and raise their two sons there.

The archaeological site of Cobá, with one of the tallest pyramids in the Yucatán (and close to Tulum), is a picturesque location for another Malleville and Bonato project. Coqui Coqui Coba looks out onto one of several crocodile-filled lakes; we were sorry to miss the reptiles' evening parade in front of the hotel.

Driving through the endless, flat, low-forested Yucatán plains, it is easy to wonder how this uneventful landscape was host to one of the so-called cradles of civilization, where the Mayans built their first well-planned cities around 750 BCE. However, part of the magic of this region of Mexico is what lies hidden around the corner. A spectacular ruin, a colorful town, or a grand hacienda—all these play their part in the mystery that is the Yucatán Peninsula.

Above, top: A glimpse of the central courtyard lake through reclaimed-wood window shutters at Plantel Matilde. Above, middle: The peaceful Calle 41 in Valladolid. Above, bottom: A palapa, or gazebo, overlooking the lake at Coqui Coqui Coba.

Right: A very early map of the Yucatán from 1616 by Flemish cartographer Petrus Bertius.

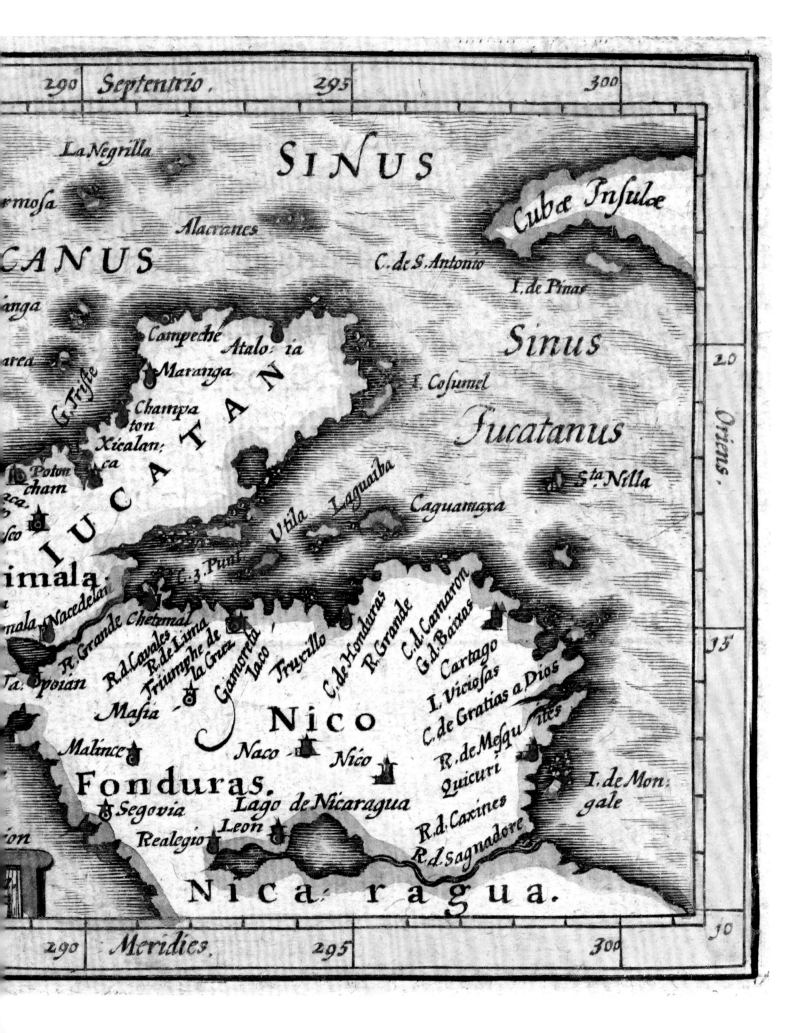

La Negrilla

SINUS

Cubæ Insulæ

rmosa

Alacranes

CANUS

C. de S. Antonio

I. de Pinas

anga

Campeche

Sinus

arca

Atalo ia

G. Trifte

Maranga

20

Champa
ton

Jucatanus

Xicalan;
ca

Poton
cham

I. Cosumel

S. ta Nilla

Laguaiba

Vtila

Caguamaxa

co

IUCATAN

mala

C. 3. Pun:

Nacedelar

R. Grande Chetumal

R. d. Cavales

R. Grande

C. d. Camaron

15

mala

R. de Luna

C. de Honduras

G. d. Baixas

Ta. Opoian

Triumphe de
la Cruz

Gamoreta
Iaco

Truxillo

Cartago

I. Viciosas

Masfia

C. de Gratias a Dios

Nico

Malince

Naco

Nico

R. de Mesqu ites

Fonduras.

Quicuri

I. de Mon:
gale

Segovia

Lago de Nicaragua

R. d. Caxines

Realegio

Leon

R. d. Sagnadore

Nica ragua.

HACIENDA PETAC

he predominantly nineteenth-century haciendas of the Yucatán are rather like old dowagers that have had "a little work done." Gracious and stately, they are poignant remnants of an earlier, more industrious era, and in recent years have been repurposed as hotels and private villas and transformed into destinations for rest and relaxation. Strung like a necklace across the Yucatán Peninsula, these haciendas make ideal bases for touring the numerous pre-Columbian pyramids of the area.

Entered from the dusty, small village of Petac through a large Baroque stone arch, the Hacienda Petac sits peacefully at the end of a graciously winding gravel driveway overhung by large flowering trees. A seventeenth-century colonial cattle hacienda, it was built on the remains of an old Mayan site and converted into a henequen plantation in the late 1800s.

The main house is rich in character, its Moorish-style features carefully preserved. Doors and windows are set into thick plaster walls and left dappled with their original paint. Kept as close as possible to their original purposes, the rooms are large and cool and include a kitchen, formal dining room, and tiny chapel, which is painted blue.

The hacienda is currently owned by Charles and Dorothea Stern, one of the two couples who bought the property over fourteen years ago when it was in poor shape. They brought in the architectural team of Salvador Reyes Ríos and Josefina Larraín Lagos, with a brief to preserve the traditional details of the property but to add modern details in a thoughtfully considered style. They too fell in love with the historic property and entered fullheartedly into its restoration.

Page 12: A winding path leads to the elegant Moorish-style facade of Hacienda Petac. Its traditional stone-chinked walls have been carefully restored.
Page 13: A hemp hammock swings in the gazebo overlooking the swimming pool, which was once an irrigation tank.
Opposite: A detail of the Moorish-style arch at the side of the main building of the hacienda, where a table is set for lunchtime meals.

After first dealing with the hacienda's structural problems, Reyes Ríos and Lagos set about transforming the spaces for hotel use—adding elegantly modern bathrooms and transforming the industrial space into residential quarters.

The machine house and storage rooms with incredibly lofty ceilings have been redesigned as grand bedroom suites, and a long 1,200-square-foot equipment room was repurposed— Josefina inventively framed segments of the original graffitied walls to look like elegant modern abstract paintings. The lush tropical gardens surrounding the buildings are outlined through tall barred windows, and the hacienda is alive with the sounds of birdcalls and running water from fountains and rills around the property. Walking through the grounds is like visiting an archaeological site, with old abandoned pieces of equipment lying amid ruined buildings laden with creeping tropical vines, or cleaned up and showcased on the lawns as large sculptural objects. Larraín planned the pools of water to cool the gardens and planted much of the garden you can visit today.

The rest of the 250-acre property that surrounds the hacienda was historically laid out like outdoor rooms, fenced in by tall stone walls. Once vegetable gardens, which supplied the estate with food, these are now small landscaped fields. A Mayan-style spa, added by architect Ríos Ramos, was inspired by the indigenous local architecture.

Fourteen years later Petac has grown even more beautiful, and its timeless restoration has now become part of the history of the place. The hacienda's size is more like a private house, and you can now rent the seven-bedroom property. To keep the feeling of privacy, it is always handed over to a single group of guests at a time, which makes the experience more like a weekend country house party. Today, the owners have extended the grounds and are busy planting native hardwood trees to reforest the land. With five-star food prepared by Mayans wearing traditional dresses called *huipiles*, it is easy to feel that you have stepped back in time to the days of the haciendas in this peaceful corner of the Yucatán.

Opposite: Used every day, the traditional Mexican kitchen, where meals are prepared for the hacienda guests, is decorated with Talavera tile.
Page 18: Color is added to the table with a bowl of freshly picked red bougainvillea.
Page 19: The main hacienda dining room is furnished with traditional Mexican furniture. The lower half of the room is painted a deep blue as a contrast to the orange walls.

*Page 20: The original hacienda waterways were
redesigned by Larraín as ornamental ponds.
Page 21: Larraín planted the tree at the end of this
courtyard a short twelve years ago, and designed a fountain
and rill to help cool the adjoining rooms.
Left: Breakfast is served poolside on traditional Mexican pottery.
Hacienda Petac is famous for the quality of its traditional Yucatán food.*

Above: A detail of a locally made hand-embroidered pillow.
Opposite: Inventively hung with ropes, this guest bed was designed by the architects.
Following spread: The hacienda's facade, lit at twilight, is warm
and inviting. Pink bougainvillea was planted to match the colors of the walls.

LA ERMITA
DE
SANTA ISABEL

*Page 29: The entry to the house doubles as a dining room. Rescued from a bakery, the dining
table was covered in a yeasty paste when Powell spotted it leaning up against a house.
Above: A series of antique Mexican cabinets in the dining room holds Powell's collection of Mayan pottery.
Opposite: A tireless antiques shopper, Powell has
accumulated a large collection of Oaxacan pottery from the 1940s to the 1950s.*

Americans John Powell and Josue Ramos are very much at the center of a creative and international group of Mérida artists, designers, and chefs, drawn from all parts of Mexico, the United States, Cuba, Latin America, and Europe. The two friends love living in the Yucatán, and enjoy nothing more than acting as cultural ambassadors for Mérida, showing visitors around and sharing their enthusiasm for their adopted Mexican home. This love inspired the creation of their company, Urbano Rentals, which offers houses owned by Powell, Ramos, and those of their friends for short-term rental.

This early colonial house in one of the oldest parts of Mérida was one of their first finds. Now owned by Powell, the one-bedroom house's exterior is painted a deep eggplant color. He dubbed his home "La Ermita" after its seventeenth-century neighborhood. Close to a local town square, it is located on one of the last remaining brick-paved streets in town.

The house needed a lot of work (most critically a new roof). Powell has completed a very sympathetic and extensive restoration—La Ermita has lost none of its original character since it was discovered as a glorious ruin over ten years ago.

The reinforced and wonderfully thick original beams in the front two rooms serve as a dominant architectural element. The entrance is now a dining room and home to Powell's impressive collection of Mexican pottery, with a rare example of an early window that opens onto the street and incorporates a built-in seat. The window had been replaced in the 1950s with a wrought-iron door, but thanks to the memories of older residents in the neighborhood, Powell was able to re-create this distinctive feature and even replace the original window bars, which were discovered languishing in the overgrown garden.

Opposite: This seventeenth-century house includes
a rare built-in window seat. The original window bars were
discovered languishing in the overgrown garden.

The dining table was covered in a "yeasty paste," explains Powell, when he spotted it leaning up against a house. It had been a baker's table, used for kneading dough. This inspired him to start a collection, and he now owns several more. A keen antiques shopper, Powell now competes with Mérida's new design-savvy arrivals for furniture, retablos, and ex-votos. This requires unusual dedication—to beat the competition, Powell gets up early in the morning and stops by the local antiques stores, sometimes twice a day.

Powell focused on La Ermita's single bedroom, adding drama by centering it with a four-poster bed designed by Ramos, with added antique finials from a local junk store. Hanging on the walls on either side is artwork by the noted Mexican artist Francisco Toledo. A strong architectural feature is the beamed ceiling, which Powell continued through the house. He added a master bathroom that includes a five-foot-square sunken bath.

Powell designed the kitchen as a separate garden room to cut down on summer heat, incorporating polished cement counters, two Bosch ranges, and under-the-counter refrigerators. He also edged the poured concrete floor with red brick to add detail to the room. A battery of saucepans hanging on a rail spanning the kitchen confirms Powell's enthusiastic embrace of the Mérida food world, where both local cuisine and imported celebrity chefs are a big part of the culture.

The garden includes a series of cooling small pools and fruit trees. Here Powell relaxes with his many dogs and chickens—the chickens became pets when he couldn't bring himself to include them in his culinary experiments. Today, La Ermita is full of Powell's finds displayed in a spare, modern way, which suits the architectural blend of old and new in this historic corner of old Mérida.

Opposite: An informal sitting room, which was added by Powell, leads
to the back garden courtyard. Sitting on the sofa is his dog
Ome, a Xoloitzcuintli, which is a hairless dog much prized by the ancient Mayas.
Page 36: An antique Mexican trastero,
or china cabinet, holds a collection of local pottery.

Page 37: La Ermita has only one bedroom, so Powell added
drama by centering it with a four-poster bed designed by Ramos, with antique
finials from a local junk store. Hanging on the walls on either side
is artwork by the noted Mexican artist Francisco Toledo.
Above and opposite: A detail of one of Powell's retablos, or religious paintings,
for which he created a shelf in this small sitting room. The floor is polished concrete.

Left: Powell designed the kitchen with polished cement counters, to accommodate two Bosch ranges and under-the-counter refrigerators. He also edged the poured concrete floor with red brick to add interest to the floor. A battery of saucepans hang on a rail above.

Above, left: Local materials are used wherever possible. Here, a sisal curtain separates the house from the garden.

Above, right: Powell became a vegetarian when he started to keep

chickens as pets. A cage keeps them safe; it can be seen through a kitchen window.

Opposite: Viewed from the outdoor breakfast area, the rest of the courtyard garden is lush and green.

CASA DE LOS FRAILES

Driving across the Yucatán toward Tulum, it is easy to miss a smaller side road leading to Valladolid, a historic old town that, while smaller and more peaceful than Mérida, has all the colonial charm and flavor of its larger neighbor. Built in 1545, using stones from an earlier Mayan town called Zaci, it is close to the beach resorts of the coast and blessed with colorful streets and good restaurants. Here, Argentinian Nicolas Malleville, who is as handsome as a nineteenth-century swashbuckling explorer, and his glamorous designer partner, Francesca Bonato, bought a house over seven years ago on the picturesque square near the historic former monastery and the church of San Bernardino de Siena. Called Casa de los Frailes, it first served as a showcase for the Coqui Coqui perfumes developed by Malleville, as well as operating as a small restaurant. However, after Hurricane Wilma devastated their Coqui Coqui hotel in Tulum in 2005, the couple took temporary refuge inland here in Valladolid.

They fell in love with this picturesque small town and decided to make it their home, eventually renovating more spaces on nearby Calzada de los Frailes, the oldest street in town, for their ever-expanding businesses. These are now a Coqui Coqui small boutique hotel, perfumerie, and spa, as well as several more stores across the road, including an old-fashioned barber's shop, a hat store, and a housewares shop, all specializing in using local, natural materials and products. Farther down the street is the showroom for Francesca's drop-dead chic accessories and clothing line called Hacienda Montaecristo, which she established with Jacopo Ravagnan, an old friend from Italy.

The house is set back elegantly on a far corner of the spacious Parque Sisal, at the end of Calzada de los Frailes. Shaded by trees, it was previously used as a nursery school—the

Page 44: Named after the priests who first owned this sixteenth-century building, today
the restored Casa de los Frailes sits on a quiet corner of the Parque Sisal.
Page 45: The grand entrance was created by merging two separate rooms. The tile floors are
original, and the room is furnished with a graceful mix of Spanish colonial furniture.
Opposite: A gauzy curtain frames the opening to the central courtyard.

property needed months of restoration and rebuilding. With just a single bathroom at the back of the garden and lacking a central courtyard, lost at some point over the years, it also needed a knowledgeable rescuer.

Realizing that he was adding to sections dating as far back as the sixteenth century, Malleville was careful to treat the house sympathetically, creating more rooms leading from the main building to form a central rectangular open space, giving access to a new kitchen, bedrooms, and dining area. With workmen filing in and out, this is still a work in progress.

The large main *sala* has high-beamed ceilings and tile floors (some of which Malleville found were original to the building). These tiles help to keep the house cool, as do the large doors to the courtyard, which stay open all year round. Malleville loves books and textiles, and on tables scattered around the room are piles of exotic fabrics, which he delights in showing to the enthusiastic visitor. This area was once two large rooms, and Malleville has retained the contrasting tile floors, which resemble bordered carpets and help define each space. Through a set of nineteenth-century wood doors rescued from an old theater in Mérida is a sizable open loggia, occasionally used as a dining room. The patio beyond doubles as a playground for the couple's older son, Leon, as well as various household pets, including a small tortoise. Here, Malleville, who studied landscape design back in his native Argentina, planted cocoyol palm trees and added potted palms and ferns.

The couple decorated the property with an eclectic mix of furnishings. This combination of Malleville's Argentinian influences and Bonato's elegant Italian style, together with local Mexican cultural references, gives the house a feeling of international chic. Every night the house is filled with candlelight, giving it an added romantic and poetic atmosphere.

Opposite: A set of nineteenth-century doors,
rescued from a Mérida theater, opens onto an open-air loggia.
Following spread: Transparent curtains elegantly
drape the loggia, which leads to a central
courtyard. The candles are lit every night at dusk.

Previous spread: A corner of the entrance/living room, or sala. *Here, piles of books, textiles,
and hanging maps, as well as plenty of chairs for visitors, reflect the couple's much-traveled lifestyle.
Opposite: Open to the courtyard, the bathroom has concrete walls
and a glassed-in shower. It was designed by Malleville to be an extremely functional space.
Above: The master bedroom was designed to be as simple as possible to stay cool in the tropical heat.
Long cupboards on either side function as storage for the family's clothes and children's toys.*

Right: Malleville's training as a landscape architect came in handy when he restored the outdoor courtyard at Casa de los Frailes, adding a fountain to cool the space. Hammocks give a traditional touch to the garden.

Above: A corner of the main sala.
Opposite: This bedroom, which leads directly
from the master bedroom, is filled with masks and toy animals.
A crystal chandelier adds a note of elegance to the space.

Fundación
de Artistas

Walking from the Parque Santa Lucía, one of Mérida's most lively and popular squares, and past shop fronts selling traditional clothing—shirt-like *guayaberas* and *huipiles*—and vivid private worlds glimpsed through occasional open windows, it is somewhat of a surprise to encounter cutting-edge contemporary sculpture inside the aged dark front doors of the nearby Fundación de Artistas. This venerable Mérida home has been recently transformed into a gallery by a philanthropic collaboration between Coqui Coqui and Hacienda Montaecristo to raise art awareness in this part of the city.

Here, the Fundación is showing an exhibition by textile artist Marcela Díaz, who was born in Mérida and exhibits her works in a wide variety of materials in Mexico, Europe, the United States, and Latin America. Her sculptures—grandly scaled, tall, and often hanging—are a natural fit for the high-ceilinged rooms and have a sense of rightness about them as they are constructed of materials local to the region. Including these works that are woven in sisal, coconut fiber, and cotton in this environment rather than in a more formal gallery enables the viewer to imagine them in a more domestic space.

The Fundación is headed by New Yorker Indira Londoño; however, Coqui Coqui founder Nicolas Malleville led the design team in restoring the former residence. There were multiple uses to plan for: primarily to transform an enfilade of rooms to create a gallery, add a small courtyard tea shop, and rework the back garden as a place for plays and musical events. Walking through these open spaces is a harmonious experience; the original colonial proportions lend themselves well to viewing artworks, and carefully selected walls have been opened up for better sight lines.

Malleville is very aware that these old Mérida houses can be repurposed in many different ways; Fundación de Artistas is a classic example of adaptive reuse. He endeavored to keep the peeling surfaces of the interiors and exteriors as they were to add to the painterly quality of the rooms, and he preserved the regional tile on the floor. Malleville has even framed certain parts of the walls as if to bring the whole of the house into the gallery experience. The resurrected central courtyard fountain cools the surrounding arched loggias filled with café tables and chairs. While cups of tea and coffee are brought to the tables, birds fly in and out, with their song adding to the sounds of splashing water.

Page 60: Reflected in a mirror is Entes *by local artist Marcela Díaz. Dating
from 2006, this three-piece set is made of henequen fiber.*
*Page 61: The inner courtyard of the Fundación de Artistas reveals the gallery's past as
a private home. Refreshments are served on the veranda.*
Page 63: The typically high Mérida ceilings showcase Díaz's Cuerda, *from 2012. The
long overscaled rope made of raw local fiber hangs naturally in the space.*
Opposite: Díaz's Meditacion, *from 2011,
is installed in one of the building's principal reception rooms.*
*Above: Seen from the entrance, the exhibition
installation shows the smooth transition from a private house to a gallery space.*

*Above: A nineteenth-century Yucatán table holds a collection of
silver waiting to be used in the gallery's small café.
Opposite:* Descendencia en Movimiento, *created by Díaz out of coco fiber over a metal substructure
in 2012, fills what was once a carriage passway through to the rear of the house.*

ANEXO BROWN

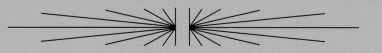

James Brown, the American painter, sculptor, and ceramicist, and his wife, Alexandra, have lived in Mexico for many years, raising three children in the middle of their somewhat itinerant bohemian artist life, traveling between Europe and, until ten years ago, a hacienda in Oaxaca. In this equally quintessential Mexican town, they founded Carpe Diem Press, which specializes in hand-printed artist books.

The couple moved to Mérida in search of more space, as there are many large industrial buildings ideally suited for artist studios and workshops in this busy commercial colonial town. At first the Browns hoped for another hacienda like the one they had left behind in Oaxaca, especially as the Yucatán is filled with the remnants of spacious henequen-empire-era properties, but as the appeal of their temporary town house grew, so did their enjoyment of Mérida itself.

This house is across the road from their main house in an old quarter of the city. The Browns consider it their "annex," having bought it when it became available as it was too tempting to pass up. For an artist, there is never too much space; James is slowly transforming it from a car-parts workshop into what looks like a living artwork—although right now it is filled with the poetic remnants of a recent party.

Unlike the usual streetscapes of Mérida, where the front facades open directly onto the street, this house has a small front garden, now planted with citrus trees. The faded gray front door opens onto an entry room with views through to a sparsely landscaped center

Page 68: From the entry, the spare empty courtyard can be seen through a glassed-in-arch.
Page 69: In the kitchen, traces of the house's past as an authomobile-parts factory
are still evident. Brightly colored flags remain after a recent party.
Opposite: A sofa, attributed to the legendary Mexican decorator Arturo Pani, was found on the
back of a truck and sits at one end of the room. The patterned tile is original to the house.

open courtyard anchored by a large ficus tree. James plans to redo at least some of the walls, but his painterly sense holds him back, as in their present condition they look like artworks. Luckily, all the floors still have their original tiles, which provide most of the ornamentation for these otherwise empty rooms.

With its tall doors and high ceilings, the house has a strong sense of scale. The largest front room is lined with chairs and is referred to as the "ballroom"; with Mérida's lively tradition of local music, there are plans to use it throughout the year. While the rest of the front rooms are furnished as bedrooms, they are plainly intended to be rooms for socializing during evening entertainments. The center room sports an immense sofa that had been found by James on the back of a truck, and that, in a stroke of good fortune, is now attributed to legendary Mexican decorator Arturo Pani. Continuing on through the house, the principal interior feature is an enfilade of rooms, leading to an unrestored back garden, which has a romantically abandoned quality.

The furnishings are from an amalgam of previous houses in New York, Oaxaca, and inherited pieces from London and Los Angeles. James likes collecting textiles, and the beds and sofas are covered with various finds from over the years. Here, he is creating domestic sculpture inside an unrestored building, which may eventually become a conceptual work in progress.

Opposite: A guest bed, draped with fabrics brought over from Alexandra's mother's home in London, is flanked by a pair of locally found lamps.

*Above: Furnished with pieces from previous
houses in Mexico, this front room has windows that open to the street.
Opposite: The Browns have built up a large collection of textiles,
accumulated during their travels. Here, antique silks and velvet furnish a guest bed.*

Opposite: A glimpse into the "ballroom" shows the original tall,
wood-framed doors and traditional tile floors.
Above: Candles add atmosphere in the evening to the sparsely lit rooms.
Page 78: James usually combines objects for their sculptural shapes rather than
for their function; however, this demi-star lantern also illuminates the room.
Page 79: The "ballroom" furnishings are carefully balanced to form a visual picture.
Here, a velvet sofa is flanked by hanging lamps and matching flower stands.

CASA BROWN

In typical Mérida style, the Browns' house opens directly from the street into an entry room, which spans much of the width of the house. Years of collecting books have turned this, their principal house in Mérida, into an extended library with bookcases rising to the high ceilings typical of this region. Twin beds upholstered in blue velvet and a carved wooden sofa from Normandy have transformed the entry room into a comfortable and useable space, with views through the house to the palm-filled courtyard beyond. In a surreal gesture, there a tree glows with deep blue lights, a remnant of long-passed Christmas festivities.

The main library occupies the central room, where art-book-filled shelves line walls that surround a long table, which can also be used for dinners with friends. Like many Mérida houses, this space forms the central core, with rooms leading off on either side.

James's and Alexandra's office, with its shelves of records and archives, is a busy space where they keep track of his artworks' travel around the galleries of the Americas and Europe and supervise Carpe Diem Press, their art book-publishing enterprise. This room looks every bit like the *oficina principal* of the hacienda they have yet to find.

Much of the furniture has been accumulated from previous houses, especially the large master bed, which was shipped from their home in Oaxaca, where the family first lived when they arrived in Mexico. Backed with a dramatic seventeenth-century European

Page 80: In the entrance of artist James Brown's Mérida home, which he shares with his wife, Alexandra, hangs a dramatic circular painting by American artist Michael Heizer, above a nineteenth-century daybed from France.
Page 81: The view through the loggia to the courtyard garden. In traditional Yucatecan style, the Browns spend much of the day here. An Italian porphyry table divides the living space from the dining area and acts as a serving table.
Opposite: When the Browns first bought the property ten years ago, they added a loggia and landscaped the garden with the help of their friend Mónica Hernández, a landscape designer.

tapestry, it dominates the room. Leading from a large dressing room, the new master bathroom is a triumph of black, white, and green tile. It is modeled on the original in the Musée Nissim de Camondo in Paris. The room was designed on site, as typically skilled Mexican craftsmen did not need conventional plans.

The Browns added the loggia, a typical Mérida-style living space they felt they could not do without—the Mexican equivalent of the sometimes pedestrian family room in the United States. Here, you can eat meals at any time of the day and sit looking out onto an enclosed courtyard filled with dwarf palm trees, shaded by ficus trees and serenaded by the songs of a fast-breeding pair of caged love birds.

Inspired by a trip to Pompeii in Italy, James and Alexandra planned a further courtyard, ending in what was once an art-storage space. It is now used as a guesthouse. They wanted to avoid the corridor-style garden popular in Mérida, where buildings run the length of the property. Pompeian houses usually had two courtyards, with a building between them and a large centrally placed arch. This second courtyard was the most logical place to add a swimming pool, another important fixture as the Mérida heat lasts most of the year. The new middle building was planned as a work space for James, but when he moved to a much larger studio, it was turned over to their three children. During the day, James works in a nearby industrial space, which has a gritty yet elegant sparseness, on paintings destined for exhibitions around the world.

Opposite: A painting by James Brown hangs on the media room wall. Here, the bed and chairs were designed and fabricated for their previous hacienda in Oaxaca—they fit the similar proportions of their house here in Mérida. Following spread: The large library, with bookcases up to the ceiling, also serves as a dining room. A sixteenth-century iron chandelier from Venice, Italy, hangs above the table.

*Opposite and above: The Browns added
steps to the roof when they built this
freestanding building in the back garden.
Many people in Mérida enjoy this part
of the house due to the views and cool breezes.
Right: The swimming pool fits
harmoniously in the rear courtyard.*

*Opposite: The seventeenth-century Beauvais tapestry of Rubens' design that
hangs behind the master bed was found in Paris. A sober set of Bauhaus furniture purchased
in Germany acts as a counterpoint to the exoticism of this room.
Above: On the master bedroom wall is a collection of personal mementos: portraits of the couple by
Alexandra's sister, Julia Condon, hang next to silver icons from Patmos, mercury-glass feet by Rob Wynne, santos
collected over the years, Mexican retablos, and a small painting by Brown to form a balanced composition.*

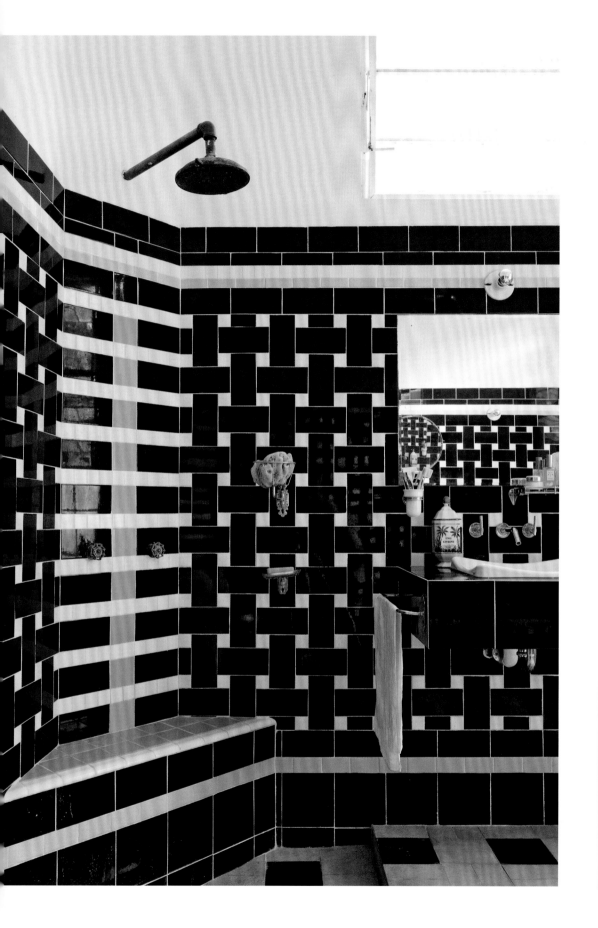

Opposite and above: The Browns added the master bathroom, which was inspired by René Sergent's basket-weave tile in the Musée Nissim de Camondo in Paris. The skill of the local craftsmen is evident here in the precision tile work.

Above and opposite: The former studio is now their son Cosmo's bedroom. It is filled with a collection of objects found in nature and an extensive collection of Native American artifacts, as well as furnishings from their previous place in Oaxaca.

Right: In what was once an art-storage area, the Browns have created a guest bedroom that includes a tall four-poster metal bed made in Mexico. The floor is polished concrete.

Opposite and above: At the end of every year, Brown installs a crèche that reflects their travels through Europe and the Americas. French and Italian figures are presided over by pre-Columbian masks and an eclectic mix of locally found pieces. Following spread: In the dramatic entrance hall, dominated by a painting by Michael Heizer, an illuminated Christmas tree adds a surreal note to this high-ceilinged blue room. In the foreground, the arts and crafts lamp from James's hometown of Pasadena was a gift from friends Robert Willson and David Serrano. Two eighteenth-century Neapolitan steel campaign beds add structure and balance.

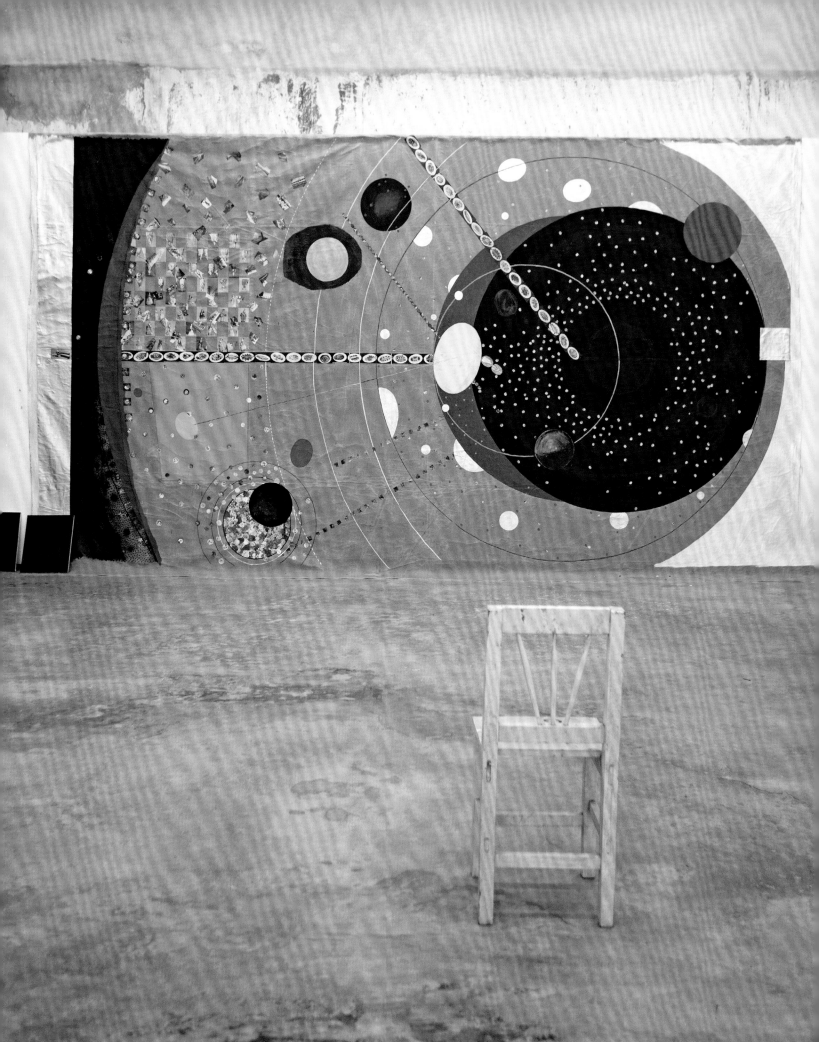

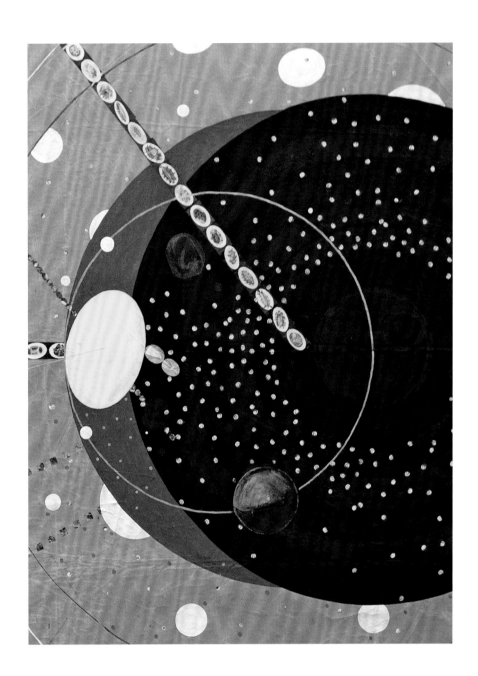

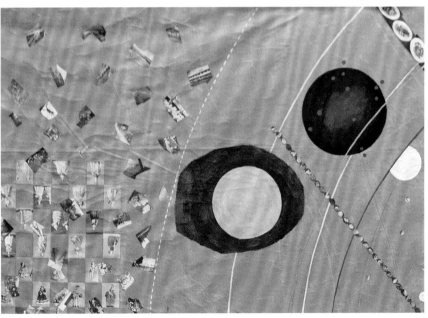

Opposite and right: In what was a vast metalworking factory, James Brown reviews his painting The Mystery of My Other House, *which explores such themes as zoning, gender, and home economics. Oil and collage on linen, this 2013 work is part of his* My Other House *series.*

CASA MESTRE

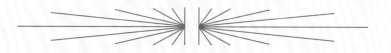

Page 104: Mestre reworked the stairs up to the roof when he added two more bedrooms to his Mérida home.
Page 105: When Mestre bought the house several years ago, he decided to keep this richly textured mural in the entry. He added a matching basket-weave lamp and a convenient table loaded with books on the region to the space.
Right: The house's original facade was kept intact because of its interesting Mexican "Deco" details. This discreet facade hides Mestre's transformation inside.

Like many houses in the historic center of Mérida, the Mexican architect Manolo Mestre's home has a picturesque but anonymous facade in line with the rest of the street. Worn exterior walls with primitive Art Deco details and a pair of modest dark green doors give no hint of the elegant balance of old and new inside this stylish pied-à-terre, originally built in the eighteenth century, with later reworkings from the 1940s.

With a busy and significant architectural practice based in Mexico City, Mestre bought this property almost by accident. Visiting his sister, who lives nearby, he decided to explore the neighborhood, with its variety of architectural styles that range from colonial to the mid-twentieth century. Admiring this house, on a whim he asked the owner, who was walking out his front door, if it was for sale. By the time he returned to his sister's place, he was unexpectedly the new owner of a house in Mérida.

Opening the front doors, you can see straight through all the rooms to the swimming pool and lush tropical garden beyond. Mestre has combined old and new very effectively, preserving the nineteenth-century interiors, including the tile floors, almost intact in the front two rooms. Then using wood slats as flooring the house transitions to a modern corridor, which has an indoor palm tree garden to one side. The high ceilings continue into the main living space, which Mestre added onto the original part of the house. Here, a long dining table, surrounded by antique nineteenth-century-style Spanish colonial chairs, becomes the heart of the room. Next to a comfortable large sofa are Mestre-designed

Opposite: A corner of the new living room, with Mestre-designed tables, where tall windows open to the first of two courtyards.

small solid wood tables that provide useful spots for drinks and snacks, decorated with carved Mexican coconut shells. A small but practical kitchen is shoehorned into a back corner of the space.

Mestre has devised the rooms as a series of indoor and outdoor areas, taking advantage of Mérida's warm climate. The combined living and dining room opens out onto a small graveled courtyard, where stairs climb up to two bedrooms on the top floor. Set well back from the front of the street, these modern rooms are farther away from the traffic noise and have views over the city. Leading from the master bathroom is a strategically placed outdoor shower, with unexpected privacy.

Downstairs, the architect kept the roof of a small garden structure intact but open to the elements, furnishing it with a large platform daybed. Here, a sheltered small pond flows through a "doorway" to a much longer outdoor lap pool, which continues down the length of the garden that is landscaped with tropical plants, including palm and banana trees. Mestre added an outdoor dining table in front of a built-in stucco banquette to take advantage of the peaceful, predominently paved garden, which feels as though it is miles away from the busy street outside. In the evening, lit with candles, the house looks like a resort in the middle of town.

Opposite: In the living room, Mestre has installed a long dining table, with Spanish colonial chairs.

Above: On a side table sits a welcoming pair of pineapples, signifying hospitality.
Opposite: The dining table is set with a collection of Mexican plates, pots, and glasses.

Right: Mestre added a long lap pool, which follows the lot's shape. Here, he created a series of garden rooms that begins with an outdoor dining room and moves through a tropical garden to a seating group in the rear.

*Opposite and above, right: Mestre has designed countless houses throughout the
resort areas of Mexico. Here, he employed one of his custom details—using stripped wooden
trunks as a screen for an outdoor shower, and for a staircase to two bedrooms.
Above, left: An enthusiastic collector of Mexican antiques and arts and crafts, Mestre
has assembled a group of Yucatecan crucifixes on a small side table.*

Left: A locally made hammock is well positioned to catch the breezes. Here, an open garden structure provides shelter from the sun, and a quiet place to read. The swimming pool inventively begins here, and flows out into the long narrow back garden. Following spread: The outdoor dining area overlooks the pool. Mestre designed the dramatic circular wall sculpture as well as the table and built-in banquette.

COQUI COQUI
COBA

Buried away in the Yucatán jungle near the ancient Mayan town of Cobá stands one of the largest properties in Nicholas Malleville and Francesca Bonato's mini chain of Yucatán hotels. Called Coqui Coqui Coba, it was built by Malleville in a playful style, inspired by the nearby ruins. These twin pyramid-like structures sit on the edge of a crocodile-populated lagoon.

From one of the dressing-room windows of the hotel's five bedrooms you can catch a glimpse of Nohoch Mul, the principal Cobá pyramid that is also one of the tallest in the Yucatán. This historic site has not yet been fully excavated from the jungle overgrowth, but you can still see its stylistic influence on Coqui Coqui Coba.

Using local stone, owner Malleville claims he didn't really follow a plan. You could call his style "*Raiders of the Lost Ark* meets Aman Resorts," as it mixes the nearby archaeological influence with the trappings of a luxurious boutique hotel. The cool, comfortable bedrooms all have mosquito nets and are curtained with natural local fabrics, while the bathrooms are filled with their own Coqui Coqui spa products.

This small hotel is hidden away at the far side of the lagoon, its unmarked dirt road reinforcing a sense of adventure. Each building sits on either side of what looks like a central rocky courtyard, which doubles as a road to service buildings at the rear of the property. A swinging rope bridge connects the bedrooms to the dining area. You can arrive for breakfast literally without touching the ground.

From the dining room, you can view the vegetable garden, where the restaurant food is grown. The garden is watered by a stream that winds down through pools stocked with tilapia from the kitchen to the lake, where crocodiles can sometimes be spotted basking at its edge. The resort's swimming pools are carved out of spaces at the bottom of the hotel buildings, while a *palapa*, or thatched pavilion, sits at lake's edge, raised above ground level to catch the evening view of the sunset. Here, you can sit with a drink and a plate of locally inspired food as you watch the sun go down to a cacophony of tropical birdcalls that echo through the jungle.

Page 123: The Coqui Coqui dining room in Cobá is an airy
open space. A large mirror with locally made hats hanging on its frame opens up the room.
Opposite: Steps lead down into one of the stone and cement swimming pools.

Above, left: Niches in the stone wall hold outdoor lights.
Above, right: The swimming pools, which are set within the building
complex, have been designed to look as though they are floating through pre-Columbian ruins.
Opposite: The vegetable garden can be seen through
the dining room window. Much of the kitchen's food is grown here.

Left: A thatched palapa, or gazebo, is an ideal place for viewing the lake and for sunset drinks. The buildings have been designed to mimic the nearby pre-Columbian ruins.
Following spread: A swinging bridge links the two main buildings together.

Above: A sisal rope, made locally, serves as a reminder of the region's prosperity in the nineteenth century.
Opposite: A guest bed draped with a mosquito net is set on a raised floor to catch side breezes.
Following spread: Malleville was inspired by the nearby pre-Columbian ruins
when he designed this hotel. Steps lead up to a bedroom.

CASA REYES LARRAÍN

Pages 136 and 137: The entry courtyard to the house, landscaped by Josefina Larraín Lagos,
was painted a typical Yucatecan blue. The centerpiece is an old wellhead, which has been turned into a fountain.
Above: The eclectic neoclassical exterior of the house gives little indication of
the size of the property. The red doors open onto an entry passage.
Opposite: A corner of the entry loggia, which also serves as an outdoor living room. Here,
furniture designed by the owners adds a contemporary feel to the space.

The old town of Mérida, spreading out over many square miles, hides its secrets well—many of its extraordinary houses are hidden behind high walls. Josefina Larraín Lagos and her partner, architect Salvador Reyes Ríos, discovered this house tucked away in the historic center over ten years ago while they were restoring big hacienda estates outside the town for their clients. Their company, Reyes Ríos + Larraín, is well known for their skillful transformation of large historic properties here in the Yucatán into small luxury hotels. In this turn-of-the-century house, they found the proportions—the high ceilings, tall doors, and the outdoor patio areas—reminiscent of the estates they were working for their clients.

Opening directly from the busy street as most Mérida houses do, the entryway has a view through the outdoor loggia to the tropically landscaped courtyard and the deep Mexican-blue of the walls of the house. A pond full of water lilies surrounds an old and unused well that continually spills water, its sound helping to disguise the rush-hour traffic noises outside. These gardens were designed by Larraín, whose aim was to re-create a typical Mérida courtyard. However, she also included a small Jacuzzi at the back of the property close to the kitchen, along with space for her family to eat outdoors.

In true Yucatecan style, most of the day is spent in the house's loggias and patios, so inside the house the couple concentrated on creating two expansive bedrooms, separated by a generous bathroom with twin showers. These graceful twenty-foot-high spaces are cooled by the flow of air through a long central enfilade that connects all the rooms. It is an elegant device that gives the house a sense of balance and proportion. In a traditional manner, every room also adjoins the patio, and cleverly designed concealed strips of skylights in the ceiling bring filtered light into each space.

Opposite: The Larraín-designed kitchen, with its unique blue-painted chimney and countertop decorated with traditional Talavera tiles from Puebla, has inspired many of Larraín and Reyes Ríos's clients. To the left is a kitchen cabinet designed by the couple.

Reyes Ríos + Larraín carefully updated the property, keeping its historic character while inconspicuously adding modern elements, including a total reworking of the plumbing and electrical systems. They furnished the house with a combination of local Yucatecan antiques as well as furniture they designed themselves.

The floors throughout are of a patterned concrete *mosaicos de pasta* tile, giving each room the appearance of a carpet of tile with polished cement borders. The color scheme is a successful balance of bright colors and neutral whites. Applied skillfully, this color palette gives the house more punch—one bedroom is a yellow ochre while the kitchen is orange and blue. Used throughout is the local *chukum* wall finish. Made with tree resin, its use dates back to Mayan times.

The enfilade opens into a generous dining room with a long table and equipal seating at one end. At the end of the house is a dramatic, much-admired kitchen. Larraín despairs of its success; she laughs, "Every one of my clients wants this kitchen!" Here, the striking blue Yucatán stove chimney is the centerpiece of the room. Along with lines of traditional patterned wall tile and a matching floor, Larraín has created an iconic room that sums up the best of the Yucatán way of life, which includes colorful regional food served at memorable meals that stretch long into the night.

Opposite: The dining room has its original mosaicos de pasta, *or cement tiles. The cupboards, or* trasteros, *were found locally. The tall doors on three sides of the room open onto the garden.*

Above, left and right: The two main bedrooms are linked by a central bathroom corridor. All the furniture,
including the bed covered in traditional Maya textiles, was designed by Larraín and Reyes Ríos.
Opposite: While most of the living spaces are outdoors, here a Mexican equipal sofa sits at the far end of the dining room.
Page 146: The bathroom is shared by both bedrooms. The sink counter is made from machiche, a local hardwood.
Page 147: A sideboard in the dining room, designed by the owners, holds Mexican craft
objects, including this display cabinet of faded paper flowers.

COQUI COQUI
MÉRIDA

The elegantly formal nineteenth-century facade of Coqui Coqui adds markedly to the gentility of Calle 55, one of many busy colonial streets in Mérida that threads through its historic *centro*. The *centro* is one of the largest and most intact original neighborhoods in Mexico, with some sections dating as far back as the seventeenth century.

Opening Coqui Coqui's broad front door feels like stepping into a Belle Époque fantasy as you pass through an oasis of glittering arrays of perfumes, scented candles, soaps, and massage oils, either housed under clear glass bell jars or displayed in vintage glass-fronted cabinets. The store and coffee shop, with its cool checkerboarded floor, is a concept designed by fashion insiders Nicolas Malleville and Francesca Bonato in 2011 as an outpost of their successful Coqui Coqui hotel in Tulum. Here in Mérida, this high-ceilinged building holds what the couple calls "fragrances of the Yucatán," as well as locally sourced clothing, jewelry, hats, and bags that round out the eclectic collection of merchandise. These include the Hacienda Montaecristo accessories line, designed by Bonato and her friend Jacopo Ravagnan.

The interior is furnished in a Mérida fin-de-siècle style, with a profusion of crystal chandeliers, gilded mirrors, and stained glass. Once past the cappuccino machine to the outdoor courtyard and the spa, you will discover a peaceful area decorated with elegant black chairs and tables.

The spa is housed in a small tiled-floor room far away from the traffic-filled street, with surprisingly spare raw-concrete walls. Nearby, an elegantly curving outdoor staircase leads up to the first floor, where twin louvered doors open to a suite of rooms, including the most glamorous bedroom in town, which features twin baths in full view of a nineteenth-

Page 148: The romantic and poetic one-bedroom hotel was inspired by Mérida's fin-de-siècle architecture.
Page 149 and Opposite: The hotel entrance displays rows of candles and perfumes in glass bottles and jars, which reflect the light coming from the street-side front windows. Called L'Epicerie, this store stocks Coqui Coqui brands as well as locally made clothing and jewelry.

century four-poster iron-frame bed. With eighteen-foot-high ceilings, the room's spirit evokes one of the most prosperous periods of the town, when sisal rope from the local agave plant dominated the world market.

Manager and co-designer Beatrice Rugai helped source the suites of gilded furniture upholstered in red velvet, the long hanging tasseled curtains, and the large centrally placed wood-framed mirror hanging on the Venetian plaster wall. With its aged glass, the mirror adds a New Orleans–style glamour and reflects the three-tiered crystal chandelier, which is anchored by a red velvet rope. Four people can fit into this single-suite hotel, although you would probably want it all to yourself. As a bonus it also comes with an upstairs sundeck and swimming pool, which overlook the town and its church spires.

Above and opposite: Stairs curve up to the single suite above. Thanks to the mild tropical climate, this space is open to the elements.

Opposite and above: The upstairs master suite features a pair of twin baths directly opposite a large four-poster bed.

Los Almendros

Page 156: In the large master bedroom of Los Almendros hangs a grand, ornate gilded nineteenth-century mirror over a console table.
Page 157: Linked by a colonnade, the interior has been configured as a series of indoor and outdoor courtyards.
Right: The Beaux-Arts exterior of the house, with its circular driveway, is an impressive sight.

Not many people dream of owning the building that was their childhood school, but famed Mexican film producer Manuel Barbachano Ponce managed to buy his in the 1960s as a second home in Mérida for his Mexico City–based family. One of the elaborate occasionally multistory nineteenth-century mansions along Reforma, near the Parisian-style boulevard of Paseo de Montejo, at one time it had been converted into an educational institution. The house had such exceptional beauty, with its plantation-style facade, that even as a schoolboy, Barbachano fell in love with it. Perhaps his subsequent career as one of Mexico's most famous producers was due to his eye for beauty—in his day he worked with Dolores del Rio and the great Spanish director Luis Buñuel.

Called Los Almendros, which translates as "The Almonds," the house has remained mostly intact since his death in 1994, and Barbachano's study walls remain lined with film awards from all over the world. They also hold his museum-quality collection of pre-Columbian pottery and sculpture, which has been exhibited as far afield as the British Museum in London.

The front gates, which have been clad with metal to screen the house from the passing parade of hopeful visitors who tend to mistake it for a museum or even a hotel, open onto a central fountain and broad circular driveway, with steps leading up to an entry loggia flanked by twin palm trees. "Los Almendros," outlined in black, is clearly visible above the arched front facade.

Once inside, past rows of white-painted rocking chairs, you can see a strong Caribbean influence in the festive mint-green walls. Here, large glassed-in doors open to a central loggia, which serves as the main living room. To beat the Mérida heat, a grouping of chairs surrounds an informal coffee table—central to where the breezes blow through the

Opposite: In the entry, a seating area is positioned to
catch the breeze that flows through the house.

*Opposite: The front porch, with its row of
white chairs and mint-green walls, has a distinctly Caribbean flavor.
Above: Inside the central loggia, a seating group includes a
table and pair of ottomans designed by the mid-century modern Mexican decorator Arturo Pani.*

house. This open living space also contains furnishings and arrangements by the great mid-century modern Mexican decorator Arturo Pani. Señora Barbachano's casa was very up-to-the-minute chic, with Pani's touches flowing through the house and into the main bedroom to the garden.

The center of the house is essentially a series of courtyards, as the next outdoor courtyard leads through to the dining room, kitchen, and breakfast room. Running along both sides of these indoor and outdoor spaces are hotel-like rows of guest bedrooms for the extended family, furnished in classic turn-of-the-century Victorian-style Mérida furniture. The dramatic master bedroom at the front of the house has many recognizable Pani touches; he was famous for his metalwork, and the master bed is a tour de force of mid-century design, topped by a starburst wall sculpture.

Outside, a path leads to a Pani-designed swimming pool and a set of pergolas that arc gracefully, designed in a South of France style reminiscent of hotels in Cannes and other filmmaker boîtes. With an enormous garden by Mérida standards, Barbachano replanted the acreage with many fruit trees, which have now grown to full maturity. To add punctuation to the garden, he carefully placed archaeological fragments along the broad paths that surround the house.

Los Almendros is shared by the next generation of Barbachanos, who include Teresa Barbachano and her architect husband, Héctor Velásquez. They enjoy traveling to Mérida as a break from their hectic lives in Mexico City. Even though it sits on a busy intersection, the house has a feeling of calm and relaxation, where sunlight rakes across the palm-tree-filled lawns and nothing is heard but the mellifluous sound of water spilling from the fountains.

Opposite: An altarpiece from the family's home in Mexico City acts as a backdrop for dining room china.

Opposite and right: Arturo Pani designed the master bed and the sculptural piece hanging above on the wall.

Above: A display of the late Manuel Barbachano Ponce's important collection
of pre-Columbian pottery sits on his office bookcase.
Opposite: The famous film producer's office showcases his awards from all around the world.
Following spread: The central courtyard is a water-filled pond,
which cools the house in the tropical heat.

CASA RAMOS ESPINOZA

About eight years ago, Mexican-American designer and painter Josue Ramos Espinoza was helping the New York artist Vija Celmins find a house in Mérida, when they came across a beautiful ruin looking almost like a hacienda lost in the jungle. This property, dating back to the eighteenth century, was filled with trees. It was like a beautiful blank slate, but too intimidating a restoration project for anyone unprepared to live there full time. Ramos loved the property, and when no one else was brave enough to buy it—he took a deep breath and paid for the property himself. Ramos figured that as the co-owner of Urbano Rentals, he was well equipped to handle his own renovations, which happily was the case.

He kept the basic footprint of the house, but added two upstairs bedrooms and a master bath. Entering the property, you can still see the magic of the original building. In the main room, or *sala principal*, Ramos installed a locally bought vintage armoire, which he painted black, and added a sofa, side tables, and lamps of his own design. Although Ramos's background is in textile design, he enjoys creating furniture for himself and his clients. The mint-blue wall color not only keeps the room feeling cool; it is a counterpoint to the black beams and furniture. Leading off the passage is a guest bedroom, where a windowless space has been transformed and made elegant with another set of Ramos-designed lamps and a tall four-poster bed. Bright colors and good lighting round out the space.

Page 172: Ramos re-landscaped the central courtyard
by adding a fountain and tropical plants while leaving the original trees.
Page 173: In the passage leading through to the main part of the house, Ramos
designed the striking white lantern and the wall sconces. The
French-style chairs were bought locally and reupholstered with Mexican textiles.
Opposite: Ramos added the master bedroom, where Ramos's dog,
Gaspar, likes to sit on the cool floor. He designed the
bedside tables as well as the sculptural piece above the bed.

*Above: A group of ceramics, a lantern, and a metate used for grinding
corn sit together on the old well in the loggia.
Opposite: In the loggia, the wall colors match the original Mérida tile floor. Ramos's
collection of mid-century plates from Oaxaca hang on the far wall.*

But it is the open-arched loggia that makes the house most memorable, with its comfortable seating looking out to a beautiful courtyard garden, and the chirping of the birds in a large standing cage in the corner mingling with the effervescent sounds of a fountain. This is a welcoming space, painted a bright Mexican orange and filled with comfortable dog-proof armchairs on an elaborate tiled floor, which is probably from the 1930s. Here you can gaze at the two large ceiba trees, important Mayan sacred trees that Ramos left in place—perhaps this is why he discovered lots of pre-Columbian stones and sculpture on the property.

The kitchen building was already there at the end of the courtyard, but Ramos added stairs leading to the new bedrooms upstairs. He also redesigned the room, adding polished concrete countertops and a bench incorporating an antique piece of hardwood. The master bedroom upstairs opens to a landscaped terrace, which has views across the town—it is said that you can see seven nearby colonial churches. In this room, Ramos employs accents of black as a foil to the bright Mexican colors in the newly tiled floor.

At the other end of the property, Ramos was lucky enough to have room for a swimming pool and a small pavilion, which he designed along with its furniture and chandelier. He hung a large mirror here to open up the space, which also increases the light from the candle-filled fixture. This expanse of water helps keep the house cool and is a popular corner for morning breakfasts.

Opposite: Ramos designed the elegant kitchen, as well as the bench,
using reclaimed wood. A painting by James Brown is the centerpiece of the room.
Page 180: The colorful loggia, seen through the courtyard's tropical foliage.
The antique stepping-stones, set without grout, add to the charm of this small outdoor space.
Page 181: Ramos added a pool and a pavilion and designed the pool furniture and the chandelier.
A centrally placed mirror gives the long, narrow outdoor space the illusion of more depth.

CASA
SERRANO
WILLSON

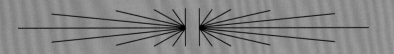

Page 182: The quiet blue exterior of the building belies the dramatic spaces inside the house. The sconces are nineteenth-century gas coach lights that have been converted to electricity.

Page 183: By the front door a wooden hat rack, with a metal tag inscribed "Los Angeles City Hall, 1930," holds the couple's collection of hats.

Right: At the back of the house, a custom mural after a Giovanni Battista Piranesi print, executed by local craftsmen, enlivens a seating niche by the new swimming pool. Most of the furnishings came from Willson and Serrano's store Downtown, in Los Angeles, including the 1920s Italian terra-cotta chair. Stairs lead up to a roof terrace.

Page 187: In the living room, a painting commissioned for the space by a local Mérida artist, Irvim Victoria, dominates the room. Next to the coffee table sits a Venetian grotto chair from the early twentieth century. The tiger silk velvet cushions on the French sofa are from Nancy Corzine.

Throughout the Yucatán, the older traditional houses generally have tall ceilings in the rooms at the front of the building, with ceiling fans to help keep them cool and doors that open directly onto the street. In the Mérida home of Robert Willson and David Serrano, their Annapolis, Maryland, architect Chip Bohl has reversed the usual order. While keeping the original 150-year-old front rooms intact, Bohl created a series of tall spaces that graduate in height and lead to the back of the house, which has been kept open to the sky. Here, he created an elegant outdoor courtyard with a swimming pool that runs the length of the property's back wall. Willson worked closely with Bohl; he traveled to Mérida every few months to supervise the execution, learning Spanish and building construction skills during the process.

Willson and Mexican-born Serrano are the co-owners of the Los Angeles gallery Downtown, which sells period and vintage furniture from each decade of the twentieth century—the house reflects this preoccupation. Moving from room to room you catch sight of spaces that seem right out of the 1920s but are filled with a mix of furniture lit by a parade of light fixtures from all decades, in particular the 1970s. Somehow this all fits together—Serrano is fascinated by the object itself, and not necessarily when it was made. He has the sensibility of an artist and feels that if the piece speaks to you, it can then have a dialogue with itself. Serrano also cites his love of foreign films as a big influence since set directors tend to mix periods. It took him two years to collect the furniture during the planning stages. Serrano furnished to measurements of the house as he did not visit until it was finished. Happily, when the containers arrived and the boxes were opened, the rooms took shape with very few changes.

Upon first impression, the overall style of their home is neoclassical. Opening the front door, you are greeted by a high row of oval windows, specifically added to hold urns from the couple's collection. Past a huge hanging blue enameled disk, which takes up considerable wall space, the house opens up to a long enfilade leading straight to the back of the property. The next sitting room has a more pronounced neoclassical mood, furnished with two large terra-cotta breasted sphinxes flanking a table filled with a collection of Roman- and Egyptian-style figurines. Most of the furniture here continues this theme; however, the space is punctuated by a dramatic pair of contemporary French wire chairs of steel and twine from Atelier Démiurge in New York.

The space continues with the first of two guest bedrooms and a ceiling-height passage to the garden that is also partly a wall library packed full of books on design and architecture. Books are also piled up in nearby rooms, especially in the bedroom called the "black room," thanks to the color of its tile floor and a hand-embroidered black-and-white Maya bedspread bought at the local Foneart store. This guest bedroom shares a Roman-style bathroom, which doubles as a powder room. Moving further along the passage, the second guest room has a Napoleonic campaign-style bed, and a small selection of the couple's photography collection, which includes work by Mexico's most august photographer, Manuel Álvarez Bravo. The polished concrete lower walls were designed to counteract moisture in this tropical climate, which tends to rise from the foundations.

As the ceilings are subtly raised throughout the house, by the time you reach the kitchen it takes a moment to notice the dramatic double-height ceiling that is befitting for the center of household activities. Here, a broad kitchen island circled by stools, all custom-designed for Downtown, adds to the impressive counter space. Willson is an accomplished chef who enjoys creating meals from the region's traditional foods.

The couple designed the tiles for the kitchen floor, which flow through the house, while the wooden cabinet doors reference traditional local doors. An oversized open hatch looks through to the dining room, where French doors open onto the back courtyard and pool— on a rocky wall perch, a large iguana sometimes joins the sunbathers. A long Italian table anchors the dining room, with a vast chandelier hanging above, which the couple found by the side of the road during an antiques store's closing sale back in Los Angeles.

The last three rooms, original to the house, once formed a separate structure. Bohl incorporated them into the main body of the house, transforming the spaces into a more private suite of rooms with the master bedroom at their center. He added Macedonia stone floors instead of tile to emphasize their separation from the rest of the house.

Outside, a large niche at the back of the property holds a built-in bench, or exedra, and a vivid mural taken from a Roman print depicting stone-making tools. Stairs lead up to a large roof terrace, where the couple spends happy hours with friends catching the northern breeze from the Gulf of Mexico and drinking mezcal in the Mérida evenings.

Opposite: The library is shoehorned into the broad passage, which runs almost the length of the house. With metal shelves designed by Willson, it is filled with an extensive design library shipped from their home in Los Angeles.

*Above: In the master bathroom, Serrano designed the locally made red limestone bath
and brought in an antique English bleached-oak chair. A striking
Chinese brass dragon hanging pendant lamp from the 1920s adds to the eclecticism of this room.
Opposite: The original beamed ceiling can be seen in a guest room, where a French
neoclassical chandelier hangs in front of a 1910 linen archery target from Belgium. On either side
of the vintage American iron bed sit a pair of verdigris iron lamps with custom black shades.*

Opposite and above: In the study, a pair of steel and twine chairs, called Stork Nest chairs,
which were found in New York at the Atelier Démiurge, are a functional part of the seating group.
At the end of the room, a pair of nineteenth-century Italian terra-cotta sphinxes,
stamped "Fabrica Altovitti, Piedmont," sit on custom-made tables.
Following spread: In the dining room, part of the original wall was left to add texture to the
space. The Murano glass chandelier was shipped over from
Los Angeles. The kitchen can be seen through a large wall opening.

Page 196: Here, in the kitchen, the ceilings reach maximum height, and are accentuated by a pair of French brass chandeliers from the 1960s from Downtown. The white oak kitchen table is part of Downtown's Classics Collection, and the appliances are from Viking. Willson designed the floor tile.

Page 197: In the second guest bedroom, a Restoration Hardware canopy bed was repainted with Ralph Lauren silver paint. The Mulholland bench is from Downtown's Classics Collection. The silver-plated table lamps are French.

Right: Reached from the kitchen and the master bedroom suite, the swimming pool was designed by architect Chip Bohl to run the length of the back garden.

casa pardo

érida has proved attractive to artists due to the availability of large commercial spaces. Like New York in the 1980s, they are easily converted from warehouses and industrial buildings. Here in the Yucatán, these studios offer both seclusion and the opportunity for artists to work toward exhibitions, especially as Mérida is well placed between the art centers of Miami and Mexico City.

With his bold environmental creations, artist Jorge Pardo blurs the distinction between art and design, often proving that a living space can be both. Born in Cuba, he moved to California when he was a child, where he has had a long and close affiliation with the Los Angeles County Museum of Art. In late 2013, Pardo was asked to design and build the LACMA9 Art+Film Lab, a portable work space that would serve as a workshop, a film-editing lab, and a place to record oral history. For this project, he reworked a shipping container, which traveled across Los Angeles as a mobile and functional artwork.

He has exhibited projects in New York and all over the world and was awarded a MacArthur Foundation Fellowship in 2010, but Pardo has now settled in Mérida, drawn originally by a large art commission to rework a nearby hacienda called Tecoh. Commissioned by Mexican banking magnate Roberto Hernández, Pardo finished this three-dimensional house sculpture several years ago. This large and involved project meant a regular commute from Los Angeles to the Yucatán. However, Pardo and his partner, Mexican-born performance artist Milena Muzquiz, and her young son only moved to Mérida full time over a year ago.

The front door opens directly into the dining room that spans the width of the house, and this sudden transition from a bustling Mérida street into Pardo's private world is bracing and unexpected—this is a house filled with playful visual surprises. The patterns and colors of its original tiled floor have been broken out by Pardo into a floating stencil design, which covers the room's high walls. A dramatic painting based on Diego Velázquez's 1656 masterpiece,

Page 200: The unusual front doors of the Casa Pardo were designed
by the artist and are used throughout the house.
Page 201: The slats in the bedroom walls upstairs are repeated in the low terrace wall.
The double-height door opening adds drama to the building.
Opposite: A richly landscaped upstairs walkway leads to a second bedroom.

Las Meninas, hangs on one wall. The long table, designed by Pardo, and the white Saarinen-style chairs add freshness to the dark room.

Beyond this, the main living space opens up to a long swimming pool and tall palm trees; it is almost entirely outdoors, except for the long stretch of kitchen counter set lengthwise into a colonnade, which leads to a two-story living space. Here, you see the dramatic verticality of the house, a contrast to the typical single-story horizontal character of the rest of Mérida.

With large picture windows opening onto the central courtyard, the living room is defined by a long L-shaped cushioned sofa running across two walls. Here, a tall room-height painted screen leads to a spectacular bathroom, where Pardo has created a space based on small and large circles. The round mirrors are placed so they reflect in an endless repetition and are bisected by a sink/cupboard island in the middle of the room.

A blue stucco spiral staircase leads up to the bedrooms, where Pardo has repeated the ceiling height of the ground-floor rooms. The cool, mint-green master bedroom has long room-height slit windows of uneven spacing that have carefully planned views of the sky and the uppermost green palm leaves of the courtyard trees below. Open cupboards painted a reddish orange above the bed hold a growing suitcase collection, and a final punch of color is provided by the bright red bedspread. Pardo uses mirrors to change the boundaries of the room spaces, and the master bathroom is defined by a twenty-foot-tall mirror that looks back into the bedroom.

A flourishing roof garden adds to the bedroom views and stretches across to another vibrant bedroom and bathroom. However, Pardo and Muzquiz can mostly be found in the central courtyard at the side of a visiting chef or two, as they love hosting big dinners at the long dining table. Recent visitors have included Italian Alessandro Porcelli, founder of Cook It Raw, and restaurant-owner chefs from the United States and Mexico, including Roberto Solis, who once worked at the world-famous Noma restaurant in Denmark. Solis's Mérida restaurant, Nectar, has become the center of what is considered the new Yucatecan cuisine. These food celebrities are drawn to Pardo's lively bohemian Mérida house to enjoy his charm, enthusiasm, and *arte de vida.*

Opposite: The elegant staircase, leading
from the central courtyard, links the two-story house.

Page 206: A Pardo-designed lamp hangs above the dining room window, which has
a view of the courtyard, lush with banana plants and palm trees.
Page 207: To the side of the pool, near the
open kitchen, a group of Jasper Morrison chairs for Ikea encircle a small breakfast table.
Opposite: A built-in set of shelving frames the bed. Cabinet doors and the
headboard feature Pardo-designed abstract patterns, fabricated in his Los Angeles studio.
Above: The master bath, surfaced with
pigment-mixed cement, is hung with Pardo-designed lamps.

Page 210: The long outdoor kitchen runs the length of the courtyard and swimming pool. The cabinet fronts are a Pardo abstract composition, while the countertops are made with a luminous blue pigment-mixed cement.
Page 211: On the hand-painted dining room walls, a copy of Diego Velázquez's
Las Meninas *adds drama to the space. Pardo designed the lanterns.*
Opposite: The downstairs bathroom was designed by the artist to have a reflective sculptural feel.
Above: A detail of the Pardo-designed wall treatment.

PLANTEL MATILDE

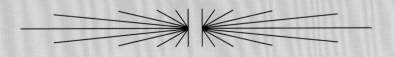

Upon first sight, Mexican artist and sculptor Javier Marín's new studio, near the small Yucatán village of San Antonio Sac Chich, is mind-blowing. The scrubby jungle opens up to a town-plaza-size square of land fringed by flowering pink orchid trees, surrounding what could only be described as a vast temple to the arts. Also a perfect square, this acropolis-like concrete building surrounds a man-made lake with a small island at its center. Here, native vegetation has been left untouched as if to make clear that this is also a temple to nature. This central island is purposely not landscaped, so the trees and plants respond naturally, drying out or becoming green depending on the seasons.

The classically proportioned entrance is on the same axis as the center of the island, with broad steps leading up on either side of it to different parts of the studio. Built to encompass many uses, the building serves as both a studio for this world-famous Mexican sculptor and as a country residence, as well as a place for students to work and learn. Constructed by his brother, architect Arcadio Marín, this studio stems from the kind of successful partnership that only a close family member can achieve—Arcadio fully understands his artist/client and collaborates with him instinctively.

A significant work of both residential and studio architecture, the building breathes the calmness and tranquility of perfect proportions. The basic plan provides two long studios situated at right angles to each other and two open spaces, a swimming pool on one side, the other side functioning as the ceremonial-style entrance. The studios are huge, of a scale with the epic nature of Javier's figurative sculpture. It is in tune with the peaceful quality of the surrounding field.

Page 214: The entry to Javier Marín's primarily concrete studio is a carefully orchestrated experience involving stepping over water to a pair of opposing staircases.
Page 215: Through tall open studio doors can be seen casts for Marín's huge sculptures, which explain the size of his studio.
Opposite: The central courtyard lake can be seen through studio windows that are hung with shutters of reclaimed wood. There is no window glass throughout the property.

The building is raised above ground level, which not only gives it a sense of drama but also provides space below for living quarters and a couple of smaller studios. There are twelve bedrooms, including Javier's master bedroom, and two kitchens—one for the artist and his guests and the other for teachers and students. Here, the long rectangular windows frame the surrounding trees like artworks, while the rooms themselves appear to have been excavated from the rocky ground in the spirit of archaeological discoveries.

In Javier's suite of rooms, which include two bedrooms for friends, the concrete ceiling was poured using planks of pine wood as forms that were later recycled into shelving and furniture. Arcadio designed all the furniture, which was made locally. In this lower level, the extraordinary textures of the walls of the building look like carefully composed paintings. Javier has used this "blank canvas" as a base for a series of charcoal drawings in the dining room.

Arcadio took a professional risk in moving to a gatehouse on the property for the three years it took to build the studio. He had left a successful architectural practice in Michoacán to plan and execute this project, named Plantel Matilde after the previous owner of the field. Arcadio doesn't have any plans to move on as he is happy to work to refine what has become his magnum opus. He claims he is channeling the spirit of the Mayans, with their geometrically proportioned civic architecture, and has clearly slipped into the spirit of the place.

Previous spread: The spectacular view from the roof shows the overall structure of the artist's studio. The island landscaping was left as natural as possible to emphasize the organic quality of the surrounding materials. Opposite: In a studio corner, Marín's huge sculptures are in varying stages of completion.

Previous spread: Included in the two colonnades that form half of the building's structure is a long swimming pool.
Right: The master bedroom is below the main floor. The roof has been formed with poured planks of concrete, while the polished floor is made from the same material, but with added sand.

*Opposite: The dining room cupboards are recycled pinewood, which
was used for pouring the concrete for the building.
Above: Marín created these charcoal drawings for the dining room walls, while
his brother, Arcadio, reworked the traditional dining chairs.
The table is of* sapote, *a local wood.*

*Below: All the living areas are partially underground. Here,
a bathroom constructed of organic materials, such as
wood and concrete, appears to have been cut into the stone.
Right: The natural rocks have been incorporated
into the living spaces like pieces of sculpture.*

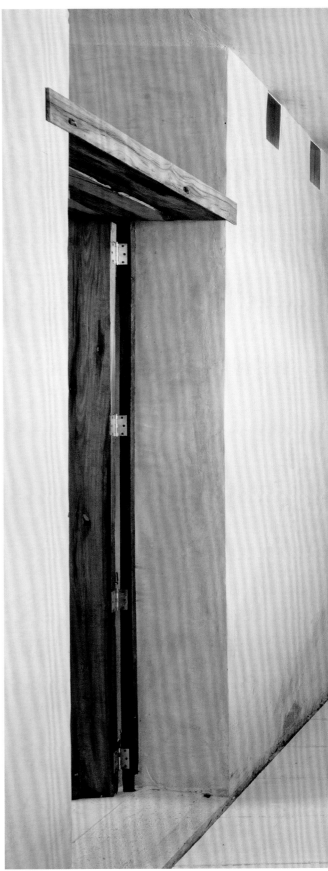

Previous spread: The flat concrete studio entrance
has been given neoclassical detailing with the addition of an intricate charcoal drawing.
Opposite: Steps lead up to the studio's roof.
Above: With lighting left over from a recent event, the second studio space seems like an endless concert hall.
Following spread: At night, the building glows in the isolated jungle landscape.

RESOURCES

ARTISTS' GALLERIES AND FOUNDATIONS

James Brown
Galerie Karsten Greve
5, rue Debelleyme
Paris, France
Ph. 33-1-42-77-19-37
www.galerie-karsten-greve.com
and
Galería Hilario Galguera
Calle Francisco Pimentel, No. 3
Mexico City, Mexico
Ph. 52-55-5546-6703
www.galeriahilariogalguera.com

Fundación de Artistas
Calle 55, No. 520
Centro, Mérida, Yucatán
Ph. 52-1-999-923-5905
www.fundaciondeartistas.org

Javier Marín
Fundación Javier Marín
Ph. 52-55-5264-8498
www.javiermarin-fundacion.org.mx

Jorge Pardo
Petzel Gallery
35 East 67th Street
New York, New York 10065
Ph. 1-212-680-9467
www.petzel.com

HOTELS, HOTEL SHOPS, AND RENTALS

Coqui Coqui Coba (and shop)
Ph. 52-1-045-984-168-1600
coba@coquicoqui.com

Coqui Coqui Mérida (and shop)
Ph. 52-999-923-0216
merida@coquicoqui.com

Coqui Coqui Tulum (and shop)
Ph. 52-1-045-984-1001400
tulum@coquicoqui.com

Coqui Coqui Valladolid (and shop)
Ph. 52-985-856-5129
valladolid@coquicoqui.com

Hacienda Petac
(for groups up to ten, minimum four-night stay)
Ph. 52-999-910-4334
www.haciendapetac.com
colleen@HaciendaPetac.com

Hacienda Uayamon
Uayamon, Campeche
Ph. 52-981-813-0530
www.haciendauayamon.com
thehaciendas@luxurycollection.com

Urbano Rentals
(Josue Ramos and John Powell)
www.urbanorentals.com
info@urbanorentals.com

RESTAURANTS

Apoala
Portales de Santa Lucia
Centro, Mérida, Yucatán
Ph. 52-999-923-1979
www.apoala.mx

Dadaumpa
Calle 55, No. 522
Centro, Mérida, Yucatán
Ph. 52-999-329-8918

Ki'Xococatl
(for chocolate)
Calle 60, No. 471
Centro, Mérida, Yucatán
Ph. 52-999-948-4738
www.kixocolatl.com

La 68, Restaurant and Outdoor Cinema
Calle 68, No. 468
Centro, Mérida, Yucatán
Ph. 52-999-924-9540

La Chaya Maya
Calle 55, No. 510
Centro, Mérida, Yucatán
Ph. 52-999-928-4780
www.lachayamaya.com

Above and below: Interiors of two of the Coqui Coqui lifestyle stores in Valladolid.

STORES

Downtown
719 North La Cienega Boulevard
Los Angeles, California 90069
Ph. 1-310-652-7461
http://downtown20.net

Fonart
Hotel Casa San Ángel
Paseo Montejo 1, at Calle 49
Centro, Mérida, Yucatán

Hacienda de Montaecristo
Calle 41/A, No. 224
Vallalodid, Yucatán
www.haciendamontaecristo.com

Takto Design Group
Angela Damman
www.taktodesign.com
angela@taktodesign.com

ARCHITECTS, LANDSCAPING, AND REALTORS

Chip Bohl
www.bohlarchitects.com
chip@bohlarchitects.com

Manolo Mestre
Estudio Manolo Mestre
Parque Via Reforma #2009
Lomas de Chapultepec
Mexico 11000 DF
Ph. 52-55-5596-0412

Mónica Hernández Landscaping
Ph. 52-1-999-738-9193
monica@jardinesnativos.com

Reyes Ríos + Larraín
www.reyesrioslarrain.com
info@reyesrioslarrain.com

Keith Heitke (Realtor)
www.haciendamexico.com
kheitke@worldstudioinc.com

Above: A horse and carriage awaits in the central square in Izamal.
Below: The authors Tim Street-Porter and Annie Kelly with architect
Manolo Mestre and artist James Brown.

ACKNOWLEDGMENTS

Tim's first introduction to the Yucatán was thanks to a magazine commission photographing a network of historic haciendas transformed into stylish hotels around the peninsula (a wonderful way to tour the region). At the now closed Hacienda Katanchel, one of the highlights was meeting the owners, the talented landscape designer Mónica Hernández and her architect husband, Aníbal González, who showed Tim the sights of their richly colorful corner of Mexico.

Several years later, architect Manolo Mestre's friends gathered together for his birthday celebrations in the Yucatán, and we joined him, along with artist James Brown, who had just bought a house for himself and his family in Mérida. We must thank them all for being a big part of this project. However, we didn't realize we had the beginnings of a book until ten years later when Robert Willson (from the eclectic twentieth-century furniture store Downtown in Los Angeles) surprised us when he told us that he and his partner, David Serrano, had just bought a house in Mérida. Thanks to his and Manolo Mestre's introductions, we started to sketch out a trip to the Yucatán.

Arriving in Mérida, we met in short order many enthusiastic homeowners, artists, and architects who went out of their way to be hospitable. These include Josue Ramos and John Powell from Urbano Rentals, architects Josefina Larraín Lagos and Salvador Reyes Ríos, Coqui Coqui's Nicolas Malleville and Francesca Bonato, and artists Jorge Pardo and Milena Muzquiz. At the Hacienda Petac, manager Colleen Casey Leonard welcomed us with some of the best food we ever have had in Mexico.

Architect Arcadio Marín opened up his brother's remarkable studio for us, while Beatrice Rugai at Coqui Coqui in Mérida provided an oasis of good coffee and conversation away from the hot and hectic city streets. James and Alexandra Brown introduced us to Teresa Barbachano and Héctor Velásquez, who entertained us for a memorable day photographing their family house, Los Almendros.

Back in the United States, thanks to decorator Sandra Nunnerley, we found our art director, Yolanda Cuomo, and her assistant, Bonnie Briant, whose skill has added an important layer to this book. Christin Markmann kept Tim's studio running with her usual professionalism and efficiency, while Ashley Likins took care of all the digital post-production.

Designer and author Florence de Dampierre gave us the benefit of her expertise and judgment, while artist Konstantin Kakanias was a constant inspiration.

Finally, thanks to publisher Charles Miers and the consummately professional Sandy Gilbert, as well as the rest of the Rizzoli team Hilary Ney, Elizabeth Smith, and Susan Lynch, who added the final polish to the book.

First published in the United States of America in 2016
by Rizzoli International Publications, Inc.

300 Park Avenue South
New York, New York 10010
www.rizzoliusa.com

Top: A new house in Mérida, designed by Reyes Rios + Larraín.
Page 1: The picturesque ruins of Hacienda San José Carpizo, just outside Campeche.
Page 2: Interior of a building at Kabah by Frederick Catherwood, print, about 1840.
*Page 3: A display case of faded flowers sits on a cabinet designed by Salvador Reyes Ríos and Josefina
Larraín Lagos for their house in the historic center of Mérida.*

2016 2017 2018 2019 / 10 9 8 7 6 5 4 3 2 1

Printed in China

ISBN 13: 978-0-8478-4826-3

Library of Congress Control Number: 2015958267

Project Editor: Sandra Gilbert

Book Design: Yolanda Cuomo Design, NYC
Associate Designer: Bonnie Briant

Production: Susan Lynch